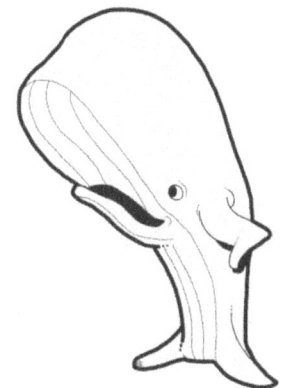

Ocean Adventures in Writing

by

Jan May

New Millennium Girl Books

Ocean Adventures in Writing
©2014 by Jan May

Education and Language Arts

All rights reserved. No part of this book may be shared, given away or reproduced in any manner whatsoever without permission of the author.

Printed in the United States of America
First Edition

Published by New Millennium Girl Books, 2014

Clipart by

Raymond Kelly at www.Spitewell.com
Ocean - http://www.whimsyclips.com/
Laura Martinez
http://www.teacherspayteachers.com/Store/Teacher-Laura
© Graphics Created by the 3AM Teacher   http://the3amteacher.blogspot.com/
http://www.teacherspayteachers.com/Store/Janelle-Web

Contents

Introduction 5

Lesson One-Create a Character 8

Lesson Two-Create a Setting 13

Lesson Three-Create a Plot 15

Lesson Four-Show don't Tell 18

Lesson Five-Write the Beginning 21

Lesson Six-Onomatopoeia 25

Lesson Seven-Write the Middle 29

Lesson Eight-Interjections 31

Lesson Nine-Write the End 41

Lesson Ten-Spice Up your Story 45

Lessons Eleven-Edit Your Story 47

Lesson Twelve-Putting It All Together 49

Cover Template 51

Ocean Animal Fact Sheets 53

Ocean Report Pages 9

Ocean Border Writing Paper 75

About the Author 87

Introduction
How to Get the Most from These Lessons

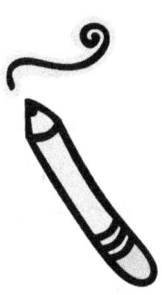

I have taught creative writing for over fifteen years-first in my own homeschool then to others. I have found that given the right tools, any child can write and love it. Stress creativity over grammar and praise every small effort your children make. Give your child the freedom to write about the topics they desire with oddball characters, fantasy settings, zany plots and all. I found out that by keeping these things in mind, even the most reluctant writer will dive into the writing pool.

This curriculum includes twelve easy lessons, with a handout for each lesson. These lessons are appropriate for children ages 8-12 years old and work well with multi-ages together. This is also loads of fun with another homeschool family, writing club, or co-op.

Students will create an ocean full of fanciful characters much like the beloved movie *Finding Nemo* as each child picks an ocean animal character to become and writes from that point of view. Each student will create a **character profile** where they will develop a personality and choose an occupation for their animal in the ocean community, such as mayor, cup cake baker, athlete, ballerina, military captain etc.

If you are doing this with one student, then have them write from a third person point of view where they know what each animal is doing. They can fill out several character profiles or name and assign occupations to them all!

Creative writing time can also be used in a unit study with more detailed ocean studies, geography, history, or art. This is a great time to study scientific classification with ocean animals or write simple research papers. Encourage your children to find fun facts to share with the family, or have a contest to see who can find the most facts. Have students keep a log of new ocean vocabulary words they find to use in their stories. They can create note-booking pages of many ocean animals or visit an aquarium or zoo.

Brainstorming with your children for story ideas and plots creates interest, and you will find the children begging for writing time. Seasonal holidays are always a fun jump-in spot for writing topics.

Write about a Valentine's Day Party: A secret message is sent to the major, and they have to figure out what it is.

Write about a St. Patrick's Day or other special day parade: The cook is missing, and the characters have to write about how he is found. Each character can draw a special parade float as an illustration for their story.

Write historical fiction about how the characters encounter pirates, Christopher Columbus, or the Pilgrims coming over on the *Mayflower*.

Include studies about different kinds of ships, both leisure and commercial, and how they affect our economy. Include sunken ships and treasure or the *Titanic*. There are lots of lessons there.

Check out my Pinterest page for ideas:
http://www.pinterest.com/janmay2012/
- Ocean crafts for kids
- Ocean food to make with kids
- Ocean unit-study ideas
- How to make writing fun with projects

Stick with the same theme for several weeks, then switch to another one when the children complete their chapter. By the end of twelve weeks the students will have written several chapters about the same character. Have the students illustrate their stories and read parts along the way. Encourage them to include other students' characters in their stories. This enhances story ideas. At the end you can put everything together by making a fun cover with the provided template. Use a three-hole essay folder with a plastic cover. These can be found at a superstore or an office supply store. Other fun ways to put a book together can be found on my Pinterest page called "Making Writing Fun": http://www.pinterest.com/janmay2012/

End the unit with a Flashlight Theatre celebration with friends and family. The children can use flashlights, turn out the lights, and shine them on the reader. Buy or make a special snack together. My Pinterest page has lots of ideas for fish and ocean foods, including clam cookies with edible eyes. These are a great hit!
http://www.pinterest.com/janmay2012/ Each child can read their stories for all to hear. This is a great way for dad and the grandparents to stay up to date on what the children are studying. It's always a highlight of the semester!

Five Tips to Help Your Child Succeed in Creative Writing

1. Don't make creative writing a lesson in grammar or spelling. This is paramount. If the critical voice becomes too noisy, it will drown out the creative voice. Your child will stop wanting to write and may resist you. As their spelling improves during spelling class, and grammar improves in language class, it will also improve in writing class.

2. Whatever they write, praise, praise, praise! You may wince on the inside over the spelling or neatness, but don't let on. They may beam at the fact they produced only one sentence in the beginning. Water your little "plants" with encouragement and watch them grow, grow, grow!

3. Let them write about what they love. Silly plots, whacky characters, made-up fantasy worlds and all. Many times a child is processing what they are learning about in life through their characters.

4. Keep tools handy that will help them succeed. Find a fun and creative writing curriculum that can help you step by step. Look for something that is easy to use and will help your child stir up ideas.

5. Give them a reason to write by starting a Friday night Flashlight Theatre or writing club. Invite grandma and grandpa, neighbors, friends, or families over to listen to the next adventure your child or group has written. Turn off the lights and shine several flashlights on the reader. Pop popcorn or serve a favorite snack. Let your child read their stories for all to hear. They will soon be motivated to write more and more. The other children may want to join in and write too.

Lesson One
Create a Character Profile

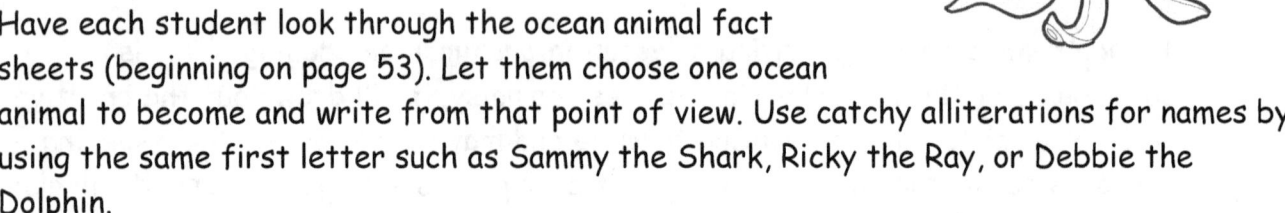

Have each student look through the ocean animal fact sheets (beginning on page 53). Let them choose one ocean animal to become and write from that point of view. Use catchy alliterations for names by using the same first letter such as Sammy the Shark, Ricky the Ray, or Debbie the Dolphin.

A good story helps the characters grow. Each character should have some weakness to be realistic. If Debbie the Dolphin starts out selfish, give her opportunities to learn how to give. If Sammy the Shark is fearful, give him a situation where he learns to face his fears and gain courage.

Students fill out Lesson One Handout-Create a Character Profile

NOTE-Lessons one through four teach prewriting and priming the pump of creativity. These are necessary parts of the writing process. Most students will become very excited during these lessons. It is important for you, the teacher, to lead the class in brainstorming ideas for the characters and create a buzz about what is happening daily in your ocean city. It becomes a community adventure that all the children will enjoy. Even the reluctant writer will dive in!

> **Activity-Ocean Animal Report**
> All professional writers engage in research. Have the students research their ocean animal and write a short science report. Use the **My Ocean Animal Report** handouts on the next page. Instruct them to include **ocean vocabulary words** they might find to use in their stories. Start a contest on who can find the most ocean vocabulary words. Let them write them out on colored construction paper and post on a bulletin board.

Notes

_____

_____

My Ocean Animal Report

What is your animal?
_____

Where does it live?
_____

Describe where it lives:
_____
_____

What does your animal eat?
_____
_____

Describe its size, color, and any special features:
_____
_____
_____
_____

How does your animal move? Crawl, swim, flip, etc:
_____
_____
_____
_____
_____

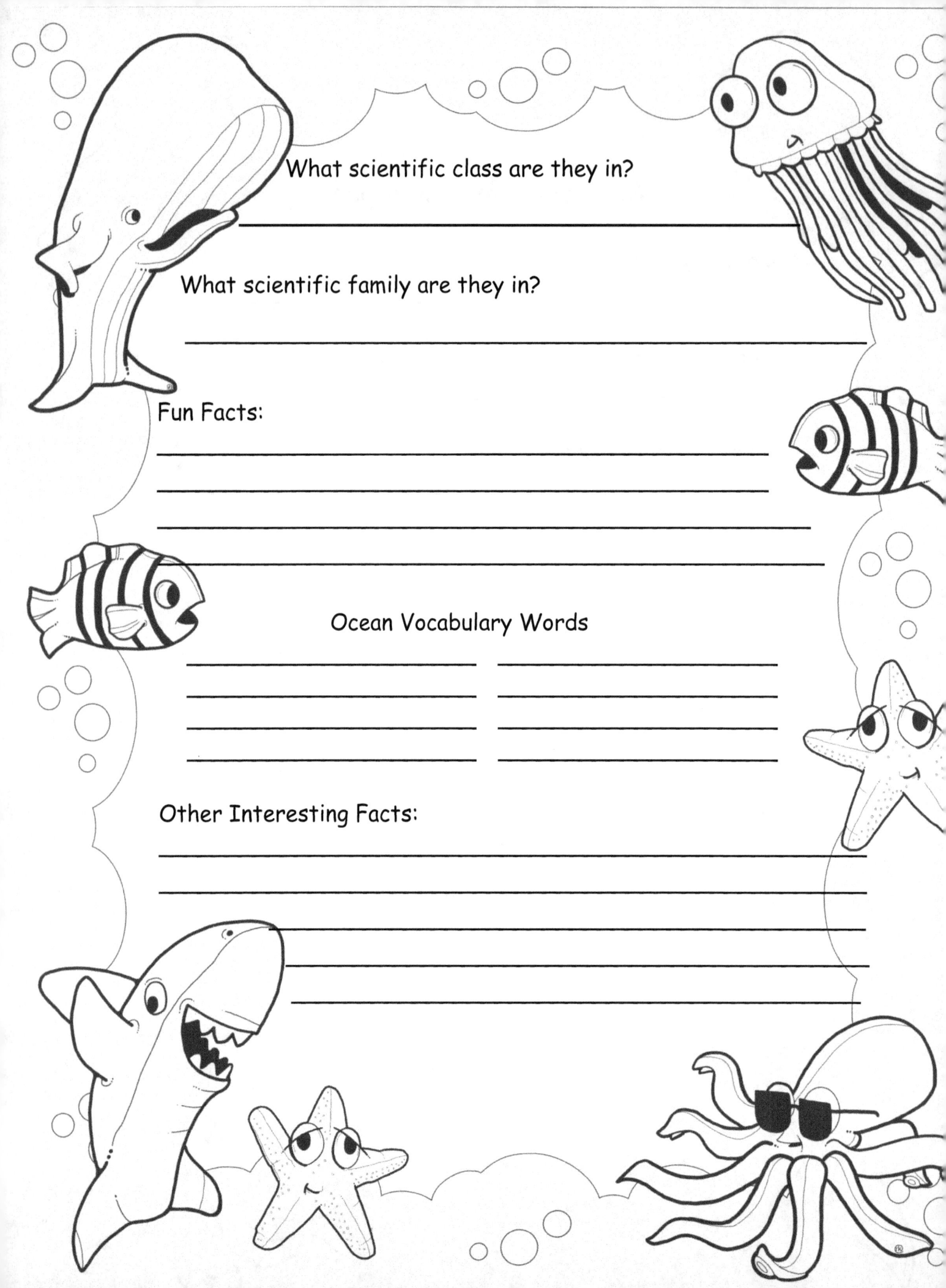

What scientific class are they in?
_____

What scientific family are they in?
_____

Fun Facts:
_____
_____
_____
_____

Ocean Vocabulary Words

_____   _____
_____   _____
_____   _____
_____   _____

Other Interesting Facts:
_____
_____
_____
_____
_____

Lesson One
Create a Character Profile

1. Choose an ocean animal as the main character in your story:
   _____

2. Is your character a girl or a boy? _____

3. Age: _____

4. Name: _____ Nickname: _____

5. What does your ocean animal character look like?

   Skin color: _____
   Skin texture: _____
   Eye color and shape: _____
   Size: _____

6. Does your character have any special features? Examples: big eyes, long nose, tentacles, sharp teeth, fins, squinty eyes, etc.
   _____
   _____

7. What is your character's job in the ocean community?
   _____

8. Where does your character live? (sunken ship, coral reef, cave, etc.) Describe it:
   _____
   _____
   _____

9. What are some things your ocean character likes to do? (Play underwater sports in the Bubble Bowl, sand drawing, sing in the Orca choir, play a bubble instrument, etc.) Make up your own!
_____
_____
_____

10. What does he or she like to eat (seaweed salad, bubble burgers, etc.)? Have fun with it!
_____
_____

11. What is your character's strength?
_____

12. What is one of his or her weaknesses? _____
_____

13. Create a personality: Choose from the list below or write some of your own traits on the lines. Circle the ones you like.

Outgoing	Funny	Serious	Loud	Quiet	_____
Smiles	Frowns	Glares	Strong	Weak	_____
Brave	Shy	Afraid	Kind	Helpful	_____
Playful	Silly	Sporty	Generous	Sassy	_____
Spunky	Sneaky	Witty	Mean	Nice	_____
Mysterious	Proud	Wise	Humble	Clumsy	_____

14. Best friend: _____

15. Favorite movie: _____

16. Favorite food: _____

Lesson Two
Create a Setting

A setting is the time in history and the place where a
story happens. It could be in a sunken ship, a coral reef, a cave, or somewhere else. It's important to describe the setting with vivid colors, sights, and sounds. Encourage the students to use their five senses.

It's also time to vote on the name of the ocean community where the classes' characters live such as Shell City, Bubbleburg, etc.

> ### Activity-Play the "Sensory Setting Game."
> Make lists of the five senses they will experience in the ocean community **one at a time** (sights, sounds, smells, tastes, touch). Have the students take out a blank sheet of paper. Tell them you will time the class as they make a list of as many SIGHTS they would see in their new ocean community. Encourage them to include adjectives. Two to three minutes are usually sufficient. Then have four or five students read their lists aloud. This gives the whole class a visual to use in their stories. Go on to the next sense, SOUNDS, and repeat the process. Go through all five senses if you have time: TASTES (might include seaweed salad, bubble burgers, etc. This is where creativity and fun flourish!)

Students fill out Lesson Two Handout-Create a Sensory Setting. Have the students fill in the blanks with their favorite answers from the above activity.

Notes

_____

_____

_____

_____

Lesson Two
Create an Ocean Setting

A setting is the place and time in history where a story happens. It could be in a sunken ship, a coral reef, or in a cave. It is important to describe the setting with vivid colors, sights, and sounds. Use all of your senses. Make a list of the sights, sounds, smells, tastes, and textures of your ocean community below.

Sights-include colors:
_____
_____
_____
_____

Sounds-include adjectives:
_____
_____
_____
_____

Smells-include adjectives:
_____
_____
_____
_____

Things with Texture:
_____
_____
_____
_____

Tastes-include adjectives:
(like **tangy** seaweed salad)
_____
_____
_____
_____

Lesson Three
Create a Plot

A plot is like writing your own recipe. Start with characters who want to reach a goal, add a few obstacles to keep them from reaching it, mix in some fun antics along the way, and help them reach their goal at the end. A good story increases the tension by *almost* letting the characters solve their problems but fail in the first attempt. The story becomes even more exciting if they fail twice or even three times.

Students fill out Lesson Three Handouts-Create a Plot (two pages)

> **Activity-Draw and Color a Map of the Ocean Town.**
> Include other characters and their stories from the class on the map such as the bakery, city hall, sports complex, etc. Students can keep their maps in a special ocean-decorated folder and assembled with their stories in a book in the last lesson. Stickers are fun too!

Notes
_____
_____
_____
_____
_____
_____
_____

Lesson Three
Create a Plot

Use the 5 Ws to create a plot for your ocean adventure.

Who?
_____
_____
_____

Where? (Describe the setting)
_____
_____
_____

When?
_____
_____
_____

What's going to happen?
_____
_____
_____

Why? (Details)
_____
_____
_____

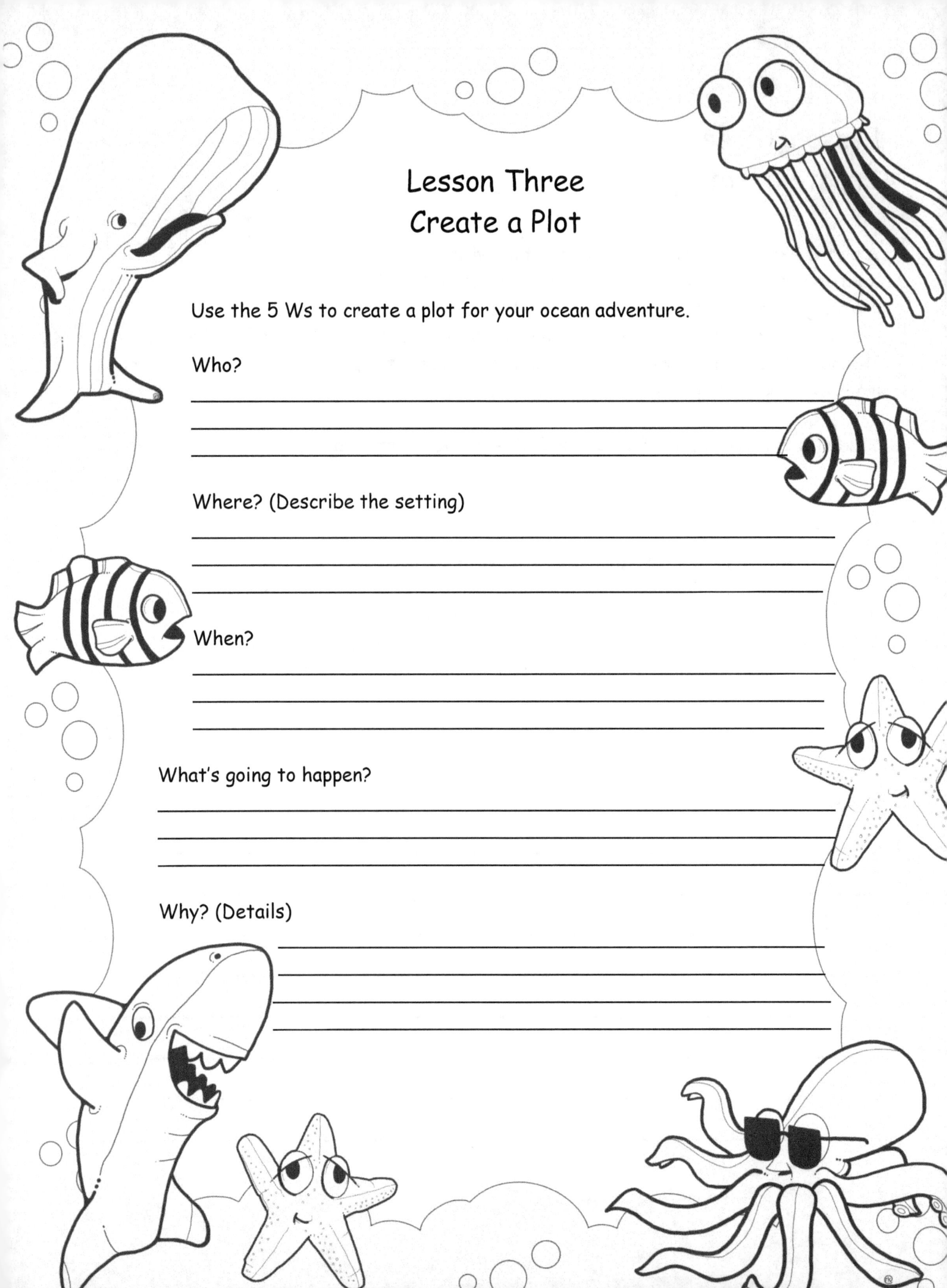

The "Build Up" Creates Suspense

In this part of the story, your character tries to solve the problem, but fails in the first several tries.

What is the problem?
_____
_____
_____

How do they try to solve it?
_____
_____

Why does this fail?
_____
_____
_____

How do they try to solve it again?
_____
_____

Do they succeed or have to try again?
_____
_____

If they have to try again–
_____
_____
_____
_____
_____

Lesson Four
The Golden Rule: "Show, Don't Tell"

C.S. Lewis, author of the popular Chronicles of Narnia series, once said, "In writing, don't merely tell us how you want us to feel. . . I mean, instead of telling us a thing was "terrible," describe it so that we'll be terrified. Don't say it was "delightful"; make us say "delightful" when we've read the description."

A strong story describes the body language of the character's emotions, making the story come alive. This is the golden rule of writing called *Show don't Tell*.

Here are two examples of someone who is afraid:

1. Patty Pufferfish swam into the dark cave and heard a sound. She was afraid. These sentences **TELL** the reader she is afraid

2. Patty Pufferfish swam into the dark cave and heard a sound. Her heart raced. She gurgled and blew up! These sentences **SHOW** her **body language** when she was afraid, helping the reader to experience her fear.

Students fill out Lesson Four Handouts-Practice "Show, Don't Tell"

Activity-Create a Setting Color Palette
Use a very large box of crayons. Instruct the students to color round circles of a color they would find in the ocean and label it. Perhaps instead of circles they can make the icons a fish, shells, or other ocean items. Then they can use the word "azure" or "turquoise" in their stories when describing, instead of plain old "blue." They can keep the color palette in their oceans folder. This also builds their color vocabulary.

Notes

_____

_____

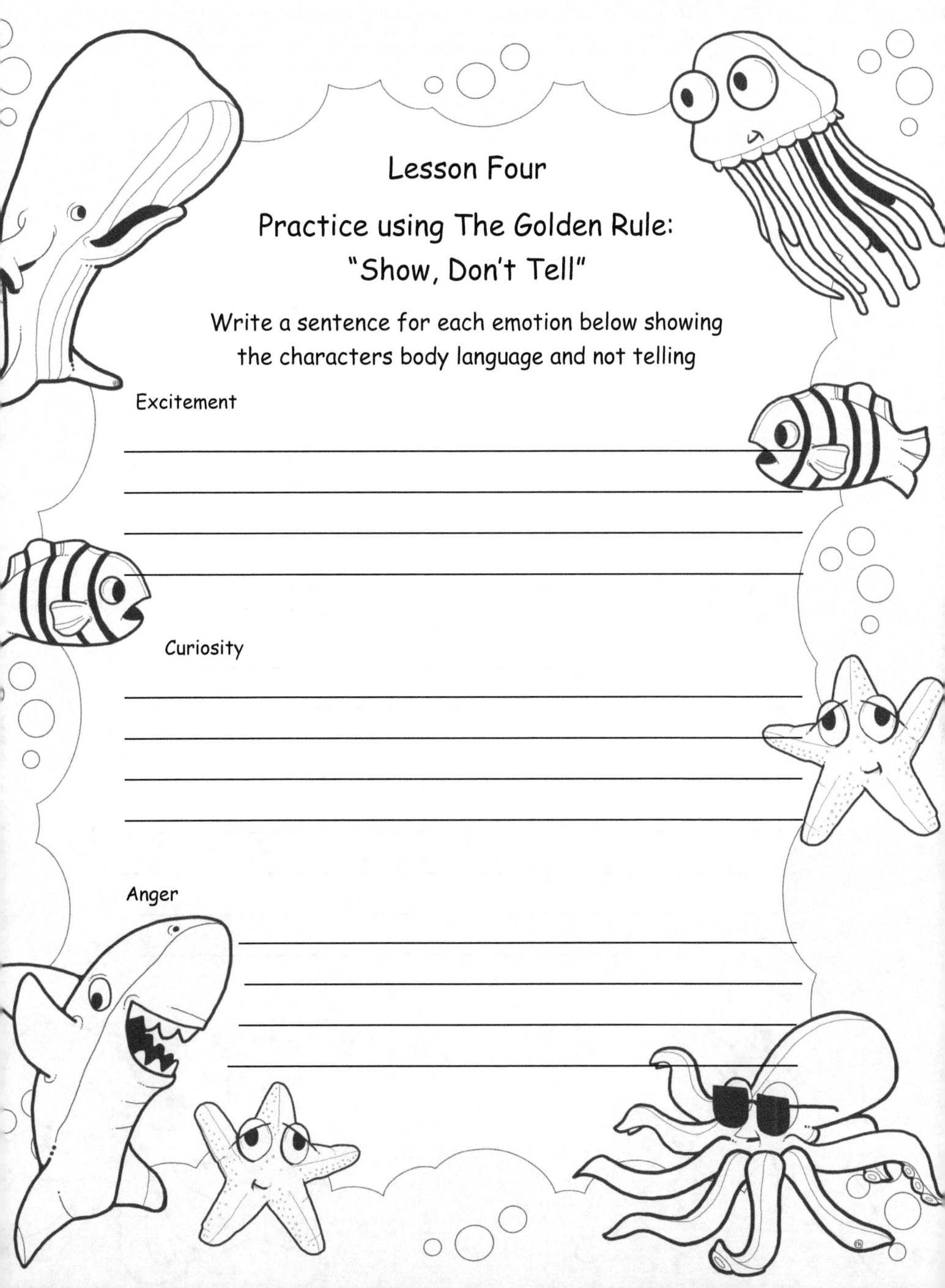

Lesson Four

Practice using The Golden Rule: "Show, Don't Tell"

Write a sentence for each emotion below showing the characters body language and not telling

Excitement

_____
_____
_____
_____

Curiosity

_____
_____
_____
_____

Anger

_____
_____
_____

Fear

_____
_____
_____
_____

Pride

_____
_____
_____

Happy

_____
_____
_____
_____

Lesson Five
Write the Beginning

Every good story has three major parts: A beginning, middle, and an end.

The Beginning: The first sentences should start the story off right in the middle of an interesting action to draw the reader in. This is called a HOOK. This should include your main character and the problem they face.

The Middle: This part of a story is where the character tries to solve the problem. It might even get worse. Think drama, drama, drama! Some writers use the one, two, three method: The first two attempts to solve the problem fail, but on the third try the character succeeds.

The End: This is where the main character overcomes his problem. If it is a fable, they can grow in character in the process. If they start out fearful, they learn to be brave. If they start out selfish, they learn the joy of serving others.
Note: Instruct the student to skip lines when writing. It makes corrections and editing easier later on.

Students fill out Lesson Five Handout- Write the Beginning
If there is time, instruct the students to write their beginnings for 15-20 minutes.

Activity-Practice Writing Hooks and Share Ideas
If you are schooling multiple students have each student write down one of the characters from the group on a piece of paper (it doesn't have to be their own) and a story problem they must solve. Collect all the ideas into a container and mix them up. Then have each student draw one idea out and write a hook according to what they drew out. Have the children read them aloud.

Notes

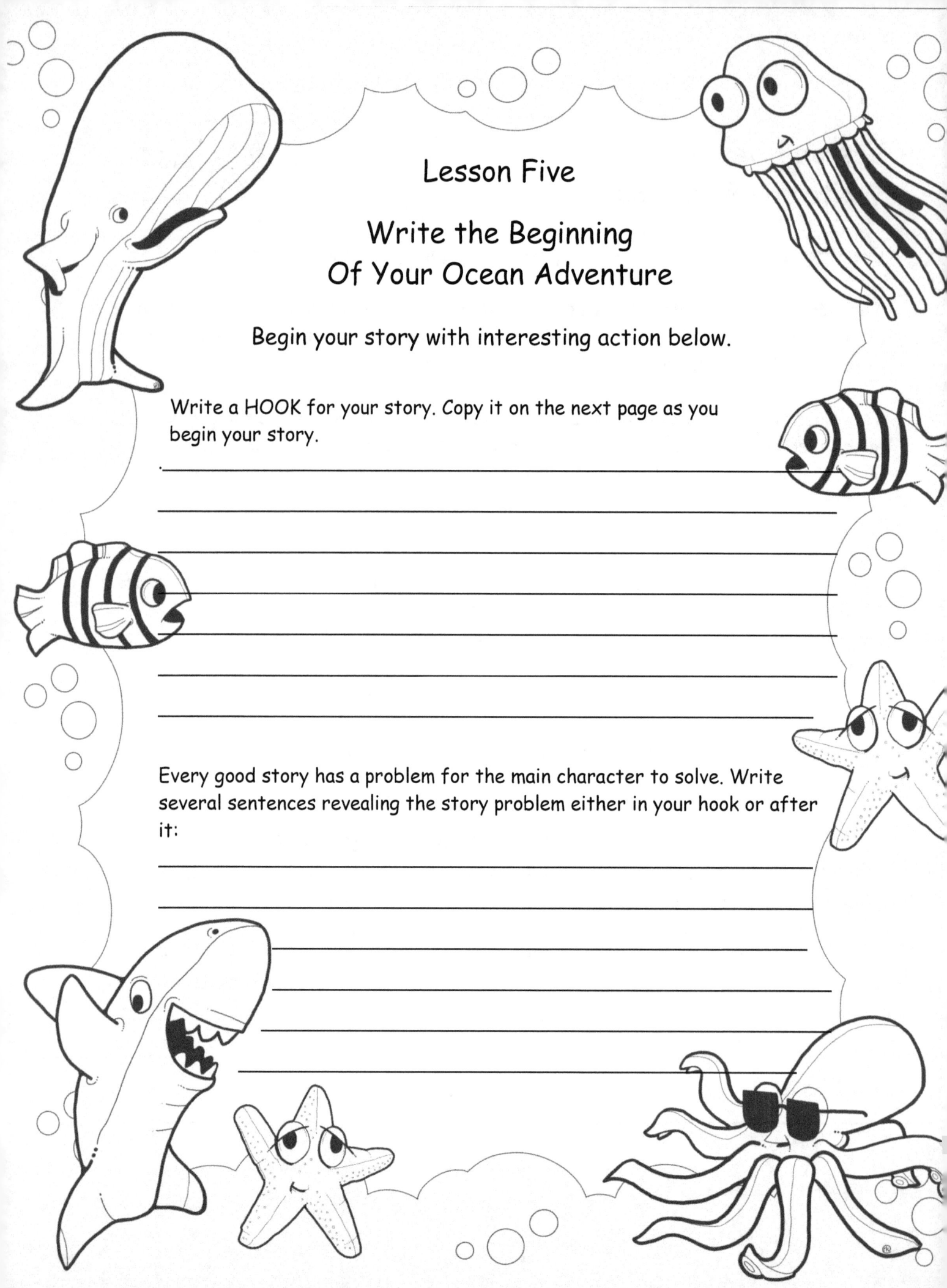

Lesson Five

Write the Beginning Of Your Ocean Adventure

Begin your story with interesting action below.

Write a HOOK for your story. Copy it on the next page as you begin your story.

_____
_____
_____
_____
_____
_____

Every good story has a problem for the main character to solve. Write several sentences revealing the story problem either in your hook or after it:

_____
_____
_____
_____
_____
_____

Lesson Six
Onomatopoeia

There are many literary tools that help transform dry writing into a story that comes alive. One of these tools is onomatopoeia (pronounced ah-nê-mœ-dê-pee-ê). This is a word that creates a sound effect that mimics the thing described, making the description more expressive and interesting. These words are fun to say and fun to read! They add sound and excitement to a story, and children will love to include them in their writing.

Examples: *Boom! Swish! Splat!*

- *Boom!* The noise shook the room.
- *Splash!* The dolphin jumped out of the water and back in again.

Students fill out Lesson Six Handouts (2): Onomatopoeia
Continue writing for another 15-20 minutes encouraging the student to include several onomatopoeia words

Activity-Word Toss Game
Copy the onomatopoeia words from the following page onto slips of paper. Tape them to round Tupperware lids. Using them as a Frisbees, have the student toss them into the box and proclaim the word when it lands inside. Example: Splat! Boom! Crash! See how many words they can get into the box. If it's too easy, move the box farther away or time the students to see how many words they can get into the box in a minute.

Notes
_____
_____
_____

Lesson Six
Onomatopoeia

Onomatopoeia is when a word's pronunciation imitates its sound, like swish, zoom, zip! These words can add fun sounds to your story. Read the list below out loud and see how they tickle your tongue.

When using these words as verbs, add "ing" or "ed" at the end: flipped, swished, sloshing, whooshing, etc.

OR use them as sound effects by punctuating them with an exclamation point. Example: Splash! Boom! Whoosh!

Circle the sounds that make you think of the ocean. Use some in your story as you write more today.

Babble	Drip	Splish-splash
Bang	Drizzle	Splat
Bash	Fizz	Sploosh
Boing	Giggle	Spray
Bubble	Gurgle	Sprinkle
Clap	Hiss	Squirt
Clink	Ker-plunk	Squish
Crash	Munch	Swish

Think of the ocean characters in your story. Choose four onomatopoeia words from the ones you circled from the previous page. Write one sentence using each word. Then draw a picture under your sentence to illustrate it.

1.
_____
_____
_____

2.
_____
_____
_____

3.
_____
_____
_____

4.
_____
_____
_____

Lesson Seven
Write the Middle of the Story

The middle of your story is where the characters try to reach their goal, but the writer puts an obstacle in their way. They should try several times but not get there. Some writers say, "Think, drama, drama, drama!"

Students fill out Lesson Six Handout-Write the Middle of Your Story
Give the Students 15-20 minutes writing time.

> ### Activity-Brainstorm Ideas from the Handout
> Let the students read what they have written on the handout, then let others give them ideas on how to create tension in their stories.

> ### Activity-Story Beach Ball
> Buy several inexpensive beach balls and write one of the questions below in each different color section with a permanent black marker. Toss the ball around the room, and whatever section the students' right pointer fingers land on, they must answer that question. If a beach ball is too heavy use a balloon.
>
> - Who is the main character?
> - Where is the setting?
> - Did they use Show don't Tell?
> - What sensory details did they use for their setting?
> - What is the main story problem?

Notes

_____

_____

_____

Lesson Seven
Write the Middle of Your Story

What is your story problem?
_____
_____

List four ways the problem could get worse when the characters try to solve it. Maybe some of the ways can be funny.

1. _____
   _____
   _____

2. _____
   _____
   _____

3. _____
   _____
   _____

4. _____
   _____
   _____

Lesson Eight
Interjections

An interjection is a part of speech that usually comes at the beginning of a sentence to show strong emotion, surprise, or excitement. Unlike onomatopoeia words, they don't mimic sound but express emotion. They are usually punctuated with an exclamation point (or a comma if the feeling is not as strong). The words in bold are the interjections.

Examples:

- **Yahoo!** We won the game!
- **Whoa!** That's a big fish.
- **Oh no!** He ate the last sardine.

Students fill out Lesson Eight Handouts-Interjections.
Practice writing interjections as comic strips. Instruct the student to continue writing another 15-20 minutes and include interjections in this next portion.

Activity- Matching Game
Use the cards on pages 37 and 39 to play the match game. Instruct the student to make 2 identical cards by making the interjections and coloring exactly the same. Then cut out the cards and flip them over. Play the match game by choosing 2 cards at a time to flip over. If they are the same, the student gets to keep that match. Count up the number of cards at the end to see who the winner is. If only one student is playing, time the student to see how fast they can find all the matches.

Notes

_____

_____

_____

Lesson Eight
Interjections

Interjections are fun to write in your story! They help to show strong emotion, surprise, or excitement. They are usually punctuated with an exclamation point (or a comma if the feeling is not as strong).

The words below in bold are the interjections.

Examples:

- **Yahoo!** We won the game!
- **Whoa!** That's a big fish.
- **Grrr!** He ate the last sardine.

Circle three interjections below that you would like to use in your story.

Ah	Awe	Boo-hoo
Bye	Duh	Eek
Fiddlesticks	Hey, Hi, Hello	Hurray
Hmmm, Mmmm	Oh, uh-oh	Oh dear
Okie-dokie	Ouch	Phew
Rats	Shhh	Tsk-tsk
Vroom	Well	Whoa
Wow	Yahoo	Yippee

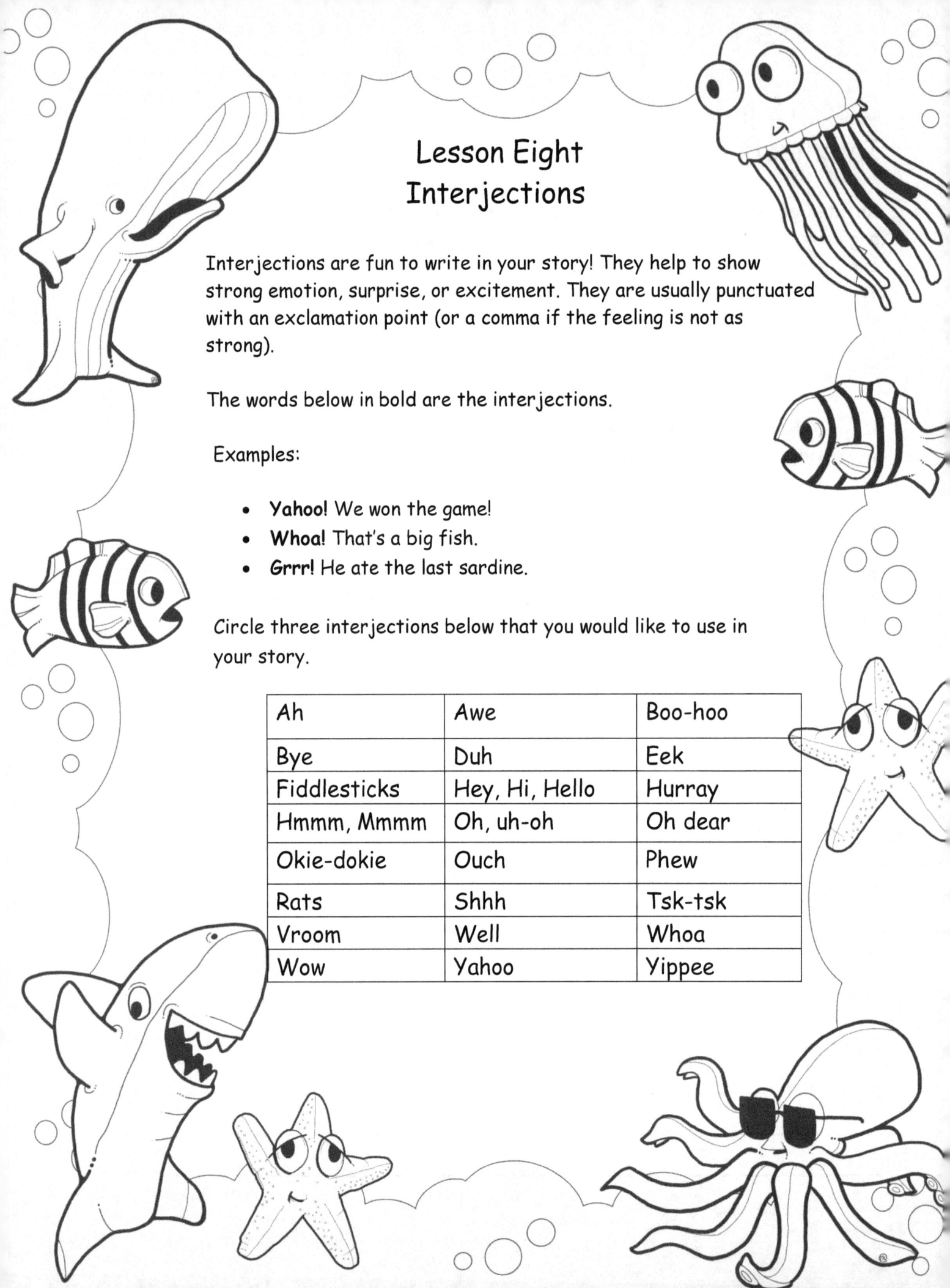

Using your characters, write sentences for the three interjections you circled on the previous page. Then make a comic strip with the cartoons on pages 35 and 36 using the interjections of your choice. Make Match Game cards with pages 37 and 39.

1._____
_____
_____

2._____
_____
_____

3._____
_____
_____

Optional - Color the picture below and draw in your character.

Lesson Nine
Write the End of the Story

You end a story when you help the characters reach their goal. If you want them to learn a good life lesson then it's also time to give them an "ah-ha" moment, when they realize they have learned something.

Students fill out Lesson Seven Handout- Write the End of Your Story
Give the students 20-30 minutes writing time. Have them number the pages.

> **Activity- Illustrate your ocean characters using the artistic** expression of dot art or *pointillism*. Pointillism is a technique of painting where small dots of color are applied side by side to form a larger image.
>
> Supply watercolor paints, plain white 8 1/2 x 11 inch paper, and Q-tips. Have students first lightly draw their character with a pencil. Then using Q-tips, fill in the character with colored paint dots. Let dry and then keep in their ocean folder or hang around the room.
>
> **Famous Pointillism Piece-** Georges Seurat painted a famous piece between 1884 and 1886 called "A Sunday Afternoon on the Island of La Grande Jatte."

Notes
_____
_____
_____
_____
_____
_____

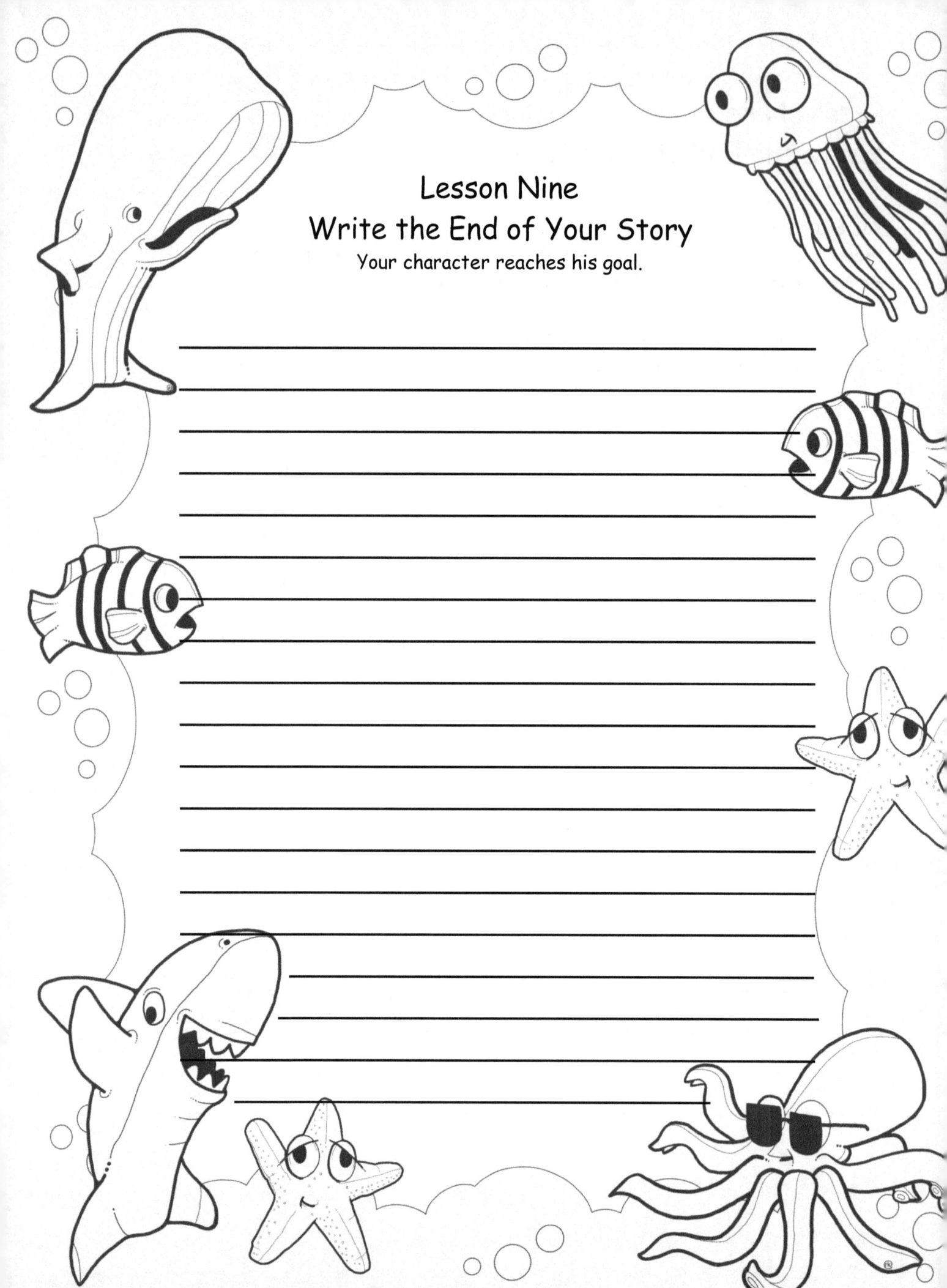

Lesson Nine
Write the End of Your Story
Your character reaches his goal.

Lesson Ten
Spice Up Your Story

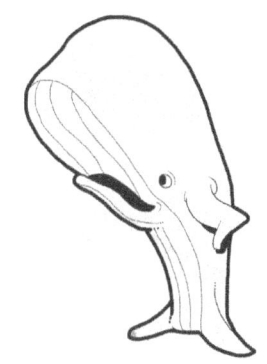

Now that the students are finished writing their story, it's time to spice it up a bit. Adding adjectives to the nouns in a story helps to create a vivid picture in the reader's mind. This also helps the reader to experience the story, not just read it.

A noun is a person, place, or thing.
An adjective is a word used to describe a noun. It can tell which one, what kind, how many, what color, what texture, etc.

Students fill out Lesson Ten Handout- Spice Up Your Story

Activity-Have the Students Illustrate
a scene from their story with colored pencils. They can add it to their ocean folder.

Notes:

_____
_____
_____
_____
_____
_____
_____

Spice up Your Story

Add an adjective in each of the blanks below for practice:

1. Shelly the Starfish smelled the _____ flowers in the _____ coral reef.

2. The _____ clam crawled across the _____ sand to greet her _____ friend.

3. The _____ Shark Brigade protected the _____ sunken ship.

4. Deena the Dolphin baked her favorite _____ cupcakes for the party.

5. Wentworth the Whale blows _____ bubbles when he is happy.

6. The two _____ angel fish swam as fast as they could when they saw the _____ shark.

7. The _____ krill played in the _____ water.

8. Larry the Lobster clicked his _____ claws.

9. The frightened clownfish hid when he heard a _____ noise.

10. The _____ jellyfish floated through the _____ water.

Lesson Eleven
Edit Your Story

Many great writers revise their stories ten to twenty times! We will only revise this story once. Lesson Eleven handouts contain an edit check list to help your students polish their stories. When they are finished they can neatly rewrite their story with all the corrections in it using the fun decorated paper on page 74.

> **Activity - Illustrate another Scene**
> Have the students illustrate another scene from their story with colored pencils. They can add that to their ocean folder.

Students fill out Lesson Eleven Handout-Final Editing and Revising

Notes
_____
_____
_____
_____
_____
_____
_____
_____
_____
_____

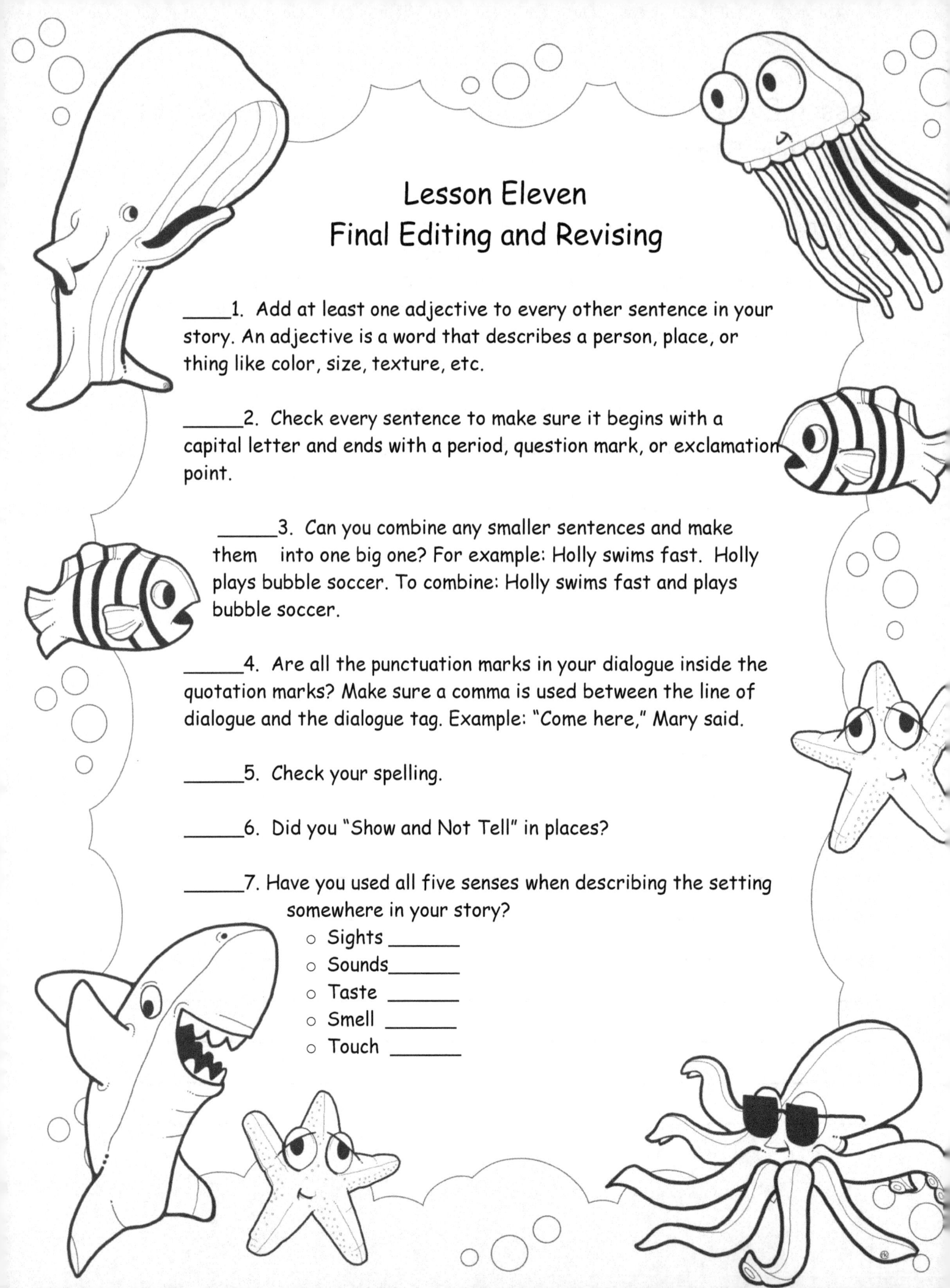

Lesson Eleven
Final Editing and Revising

_____1. Add at least one adjective to every other sentence in your story. An adjective is a word that describes a person, place, or thing like color, size, texture, etc.

_____2. Check every sentence to make sure it begins with a capital letter and ends with a period, question mark, or exclamation point.

_____3. Can you combine any smaller sentences and make them into one big one? For example: Holly swims fast. Holly plays bubble soccer. To combine: Holly swims fast and plays bubble soccer.

_____4. Are all the punctuation marks in your dialogue inside the quotation marks? Make sure a comma is used between the line of dialogue and the dialogue tag. Example: "Come here," Mary said.

_____5. Check your spelling.

_____6. Did you "Show and Not Tell" in places?

_____7. Have you used all five senses when describing the setting somewhere in your story?
- Sights _____
- Sounds_____
- Taste _____
- Smell _____
- Touch _____

Lesson Twelve
Put It All Together

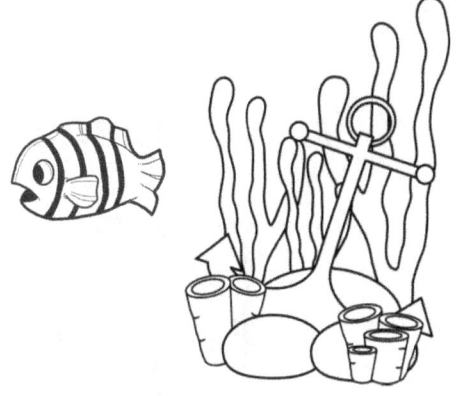

Give each student a cover page template to fill in provided on page 51. Use a three-hole punch and punch all the illustrations and cover. Instruct them to number the pages, assemble the story and any illustrations they have drawn into a plastic essay binder. These can be found at a superstore or office supply store.

This may take the whole class period. Plan the Flashlight Theater for the following writing time.

Activity-Flashlight Theater
Turn all the lights out in a room and flash several flashlights on the reader as students take turns reading their stories. The students can sit at a table or on a living room chair. For fun cut out a large square in a big box and make a TV and read behind it. Paint or decorate it with stars and glitter. This is always a highlight! Share good flashlight behavior beforehand such as: No flashing in anyone's eyes or waving them around to make fun patterns on the wall. Invite grandparents, cousins, other families, or friends to be in the audience. Make popcorn!

Notes

_____
_____
_____
_____
_____
_____

Flashlight Theater

Savory Popcorn Recipe:

- Use microwave popcorn or pop your own!
- Drizzle melted butter over the top and toss
- Sprinkle on garlic powder
- Parmesan cheese
- Almonds or walnuts
- Chili powder (optional)
- Toss together

Sticky Marshmallow Popcorn Recipe:

- Pop 3 bags of microwave popcorn – remove the seeds and dump in a large bowl
- In another bowel microwave 2 sticks of butter, 16 oz bag of mini marshmallows and 1 cup of brown sugar for 2 ½ minutes. Stir and microwave for another minute. Repeat until melted.
- Pour over popcorn and stir. Enjoy! ☺

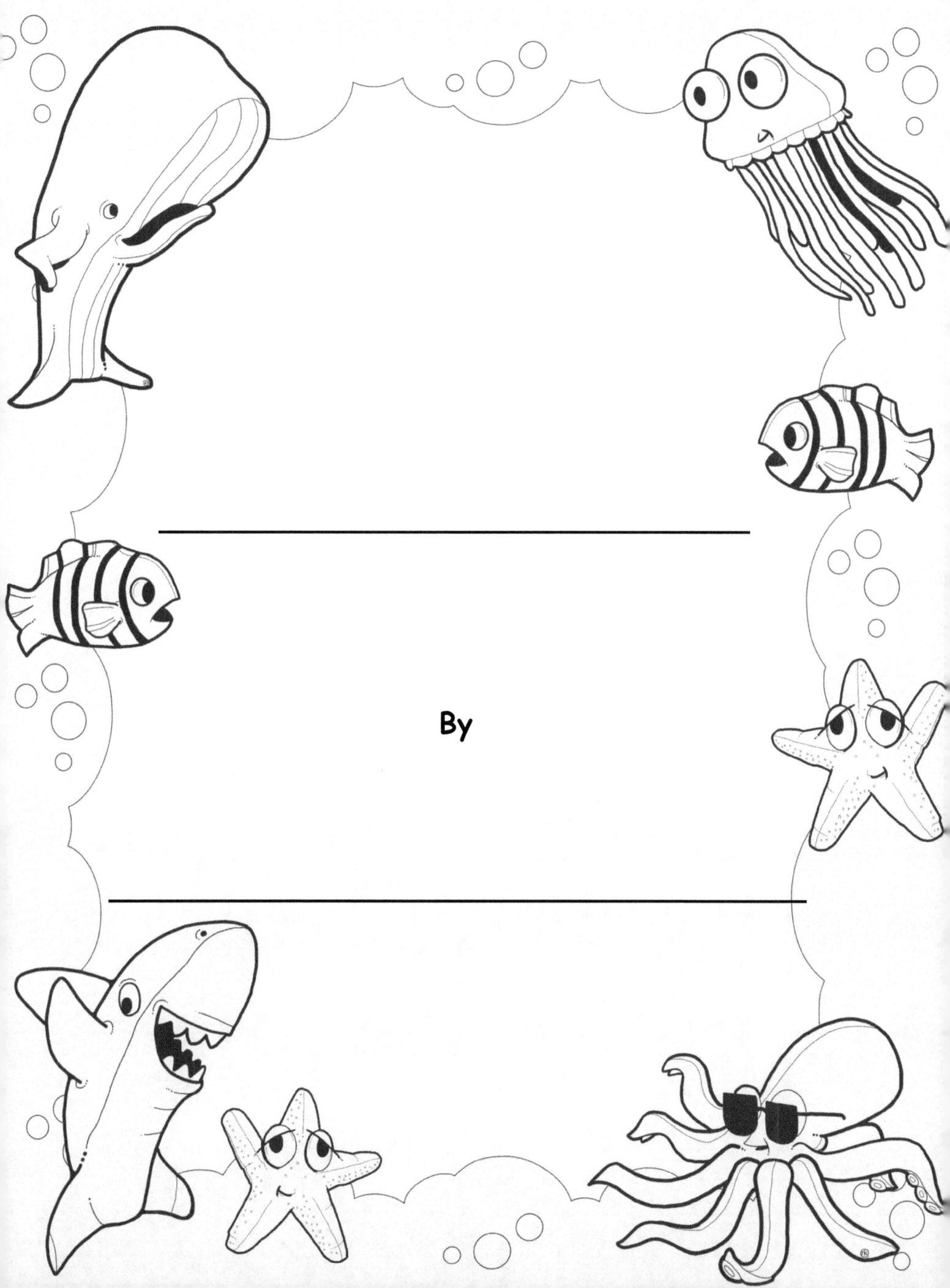

By

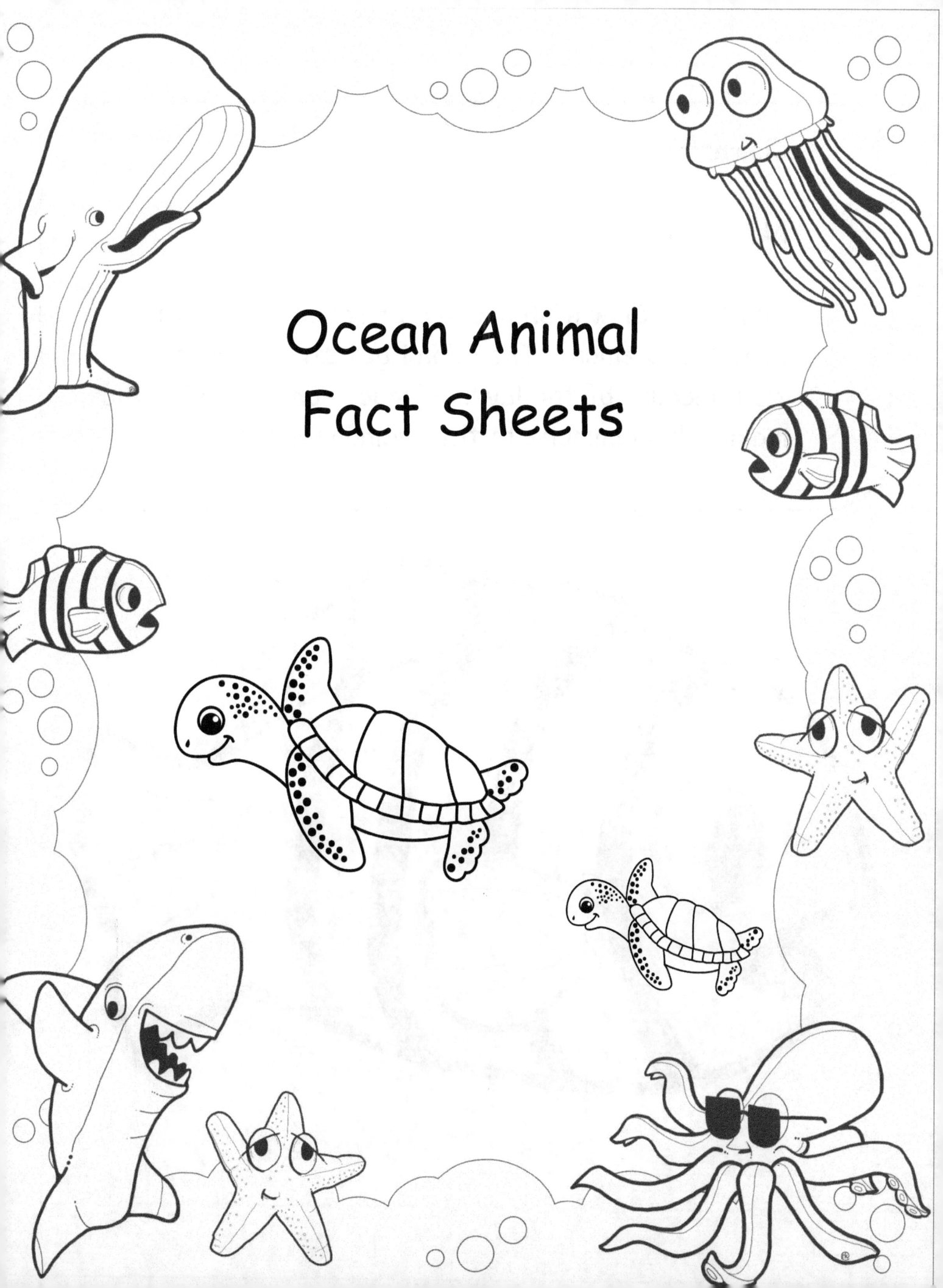

Clownfish

Native of the Indian and Pacific oceans.

Fun Fact- Clownfish live in a poisonous sea plant called an anemone. They don't get stung like other fish because of the layer of mucus on their skin that makes them immune to the anemone's stings.

Jellyfish

Native of the world's oceans.

Fun Fact-A group of jellyfish is called a smack. Some jellyfish are bigger than a human, and others are as small as a pinhead.

Octopus

Native of the oceans of the world. They live in sea caves, crevices on the sea floor, or holes they dig under large rocks.

Fun Fact- Octopuses are excellent climbers. They have suction cups under their tentacles that help them stick to everything.

Leopard Seal

Native of frigid Antarctic and sub-Antarctic waters.

Fun Fact- Leopard seals are earless seals. Their bodies are insulated from frigid waters by a thick layer of fat known as blubber.

Orca Whale

Native of the oceans of the world, but prefer coastal waters and cooler regions.

Fun Fact- Whales make a wide variety of communicative sounds, and each pod (family) has distinctive noises that its members recognize even at a distance.

Sea Turtle

Native of all warm and mild ocean waters throughout the world and migrate hundreds of miles between nesting and feeding grounds

Fun Fact- *Sea turtles have special glands, which help remove salt from the water they drink. Green sea turtles can stay under water for as long as five hours!*

Squid

Native of the oceans of the world. Some species like warm tropical temperatures. and others like cooler waters.

Fun Facts- Squid are color blind, but they have excellent eyesight. They are able to see both in the shallow and deeper water. Squid have the ability to see in a range of 360 degrees in the day or night.

Shark

Native of the oceans of the world. Some sharks have even been found in rivers and inner coastal waters.

Fun Fact-Sharks never run out of teeth. If one is lost, another spins forward from the rows and rows of backup teeth.

Starfish

Native of the world's oceans.

Fun Fact-The starfish has an eye at the tip of each arm and can grow a whole new body with just one arm.

Krill

Native of all the oceans of the world.

Fun Fact - Krill travel in swarms primarily as a defense method to confuse predators that would pick out single krill. The lifespan of a krill is typically 10 years, 6 years on average. They grow to a length of $2\frac{1}{2}$ inches (6 centimeters), and weigh up to .07 ounces (2 grams).

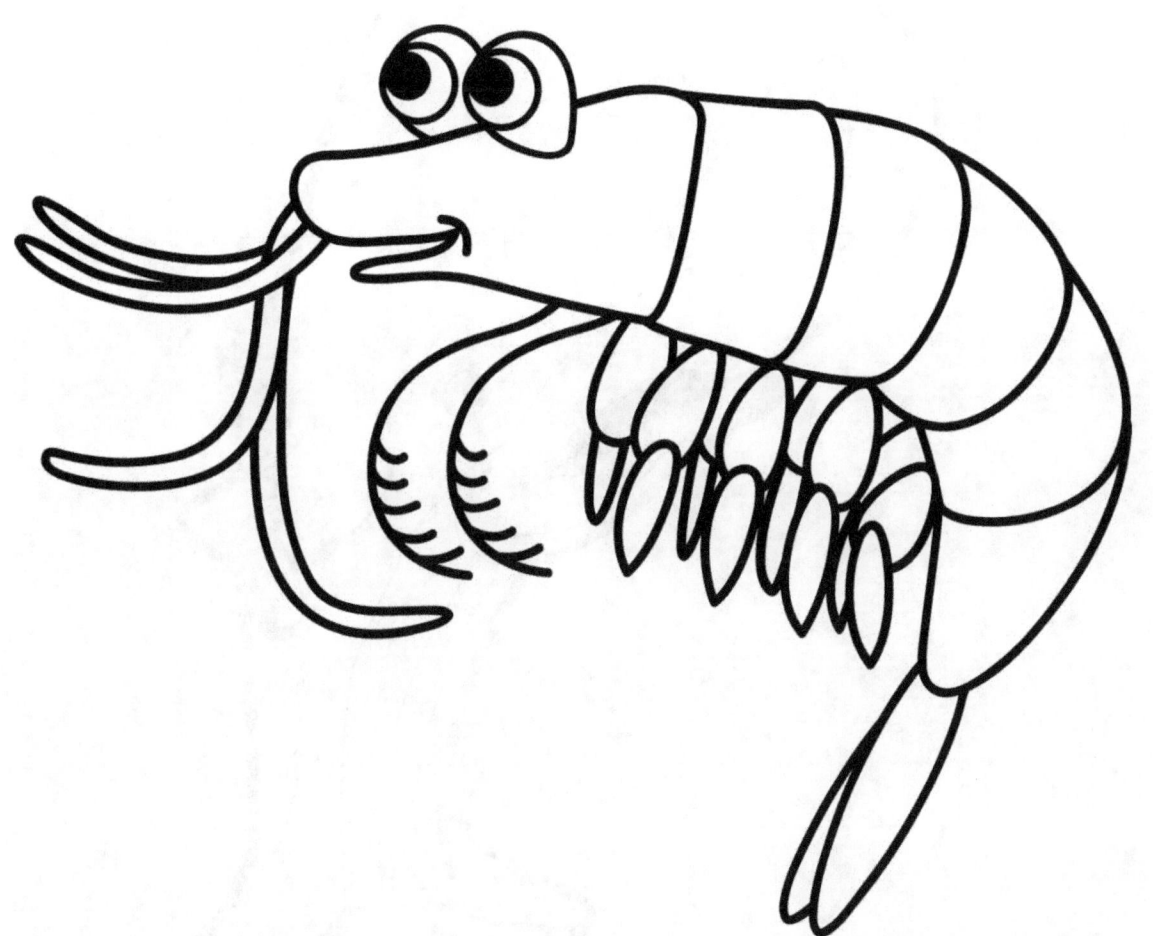

Sperm Whale

Native of the oceans of the world.

Fun Fact - Sperm whales have huge heads (40% of the body length) and possess the largest brain of any creature that has ever lived on Earth.

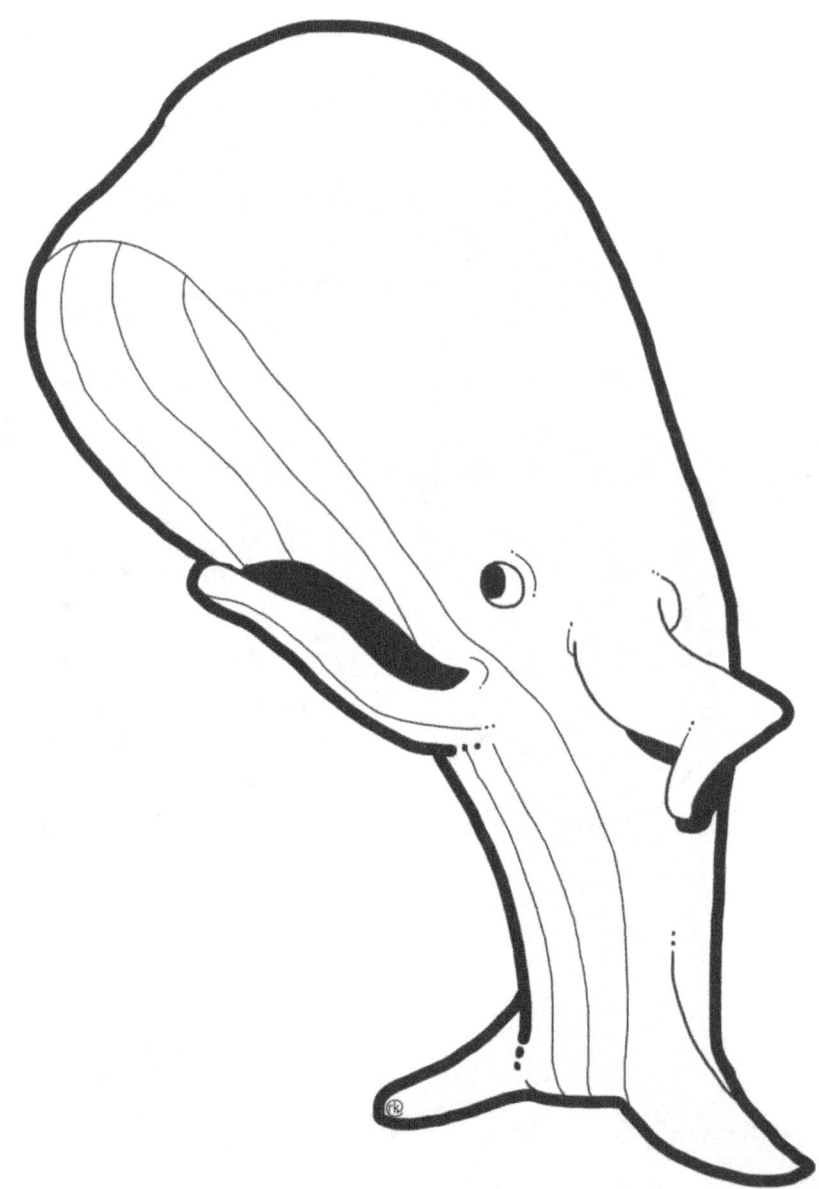

Dolphin

Native of the oceans of the world and in some rivers.

Fun Fact - When a dolphin is sick or injured, its cries of distress summon immediate aid from other dolphins, who try to support it to the surface so that it can breathe.

Walrus

Native of shallow ice shelves in the Arctic Ocean. The biggest walrus population lives in the Pacific Ocean in the summers in northern Alaska, and winters in Siberia! A smaller population of Atlantic walruses lives in the Canadian Arctic Ocean.

Fun Fact- *Walruses' tusks are actually long canine teeth. They can get up to 3 feet (1 meter) in length.*

Crab

Native to the oceans of the world, river beds, lakes, under rocks and deep holes in the sand.

Fun Fact- Crabs typically walk sideways. They are invertebrates (animals without a backbone). Their hard exoskeleton protects them from predators and provides support for their bodies.

Pufferfish

Native to tropical and subtropical ocean waters, but some species live in fresh water.

Fun Fact- Pufferfish inflate into a ball shape to evade predators. Also known as blowfish, these clumsy swimmers fill their elastic stomachs with enormous amounts of water (sometimes air) and can blow themselves up to many times beyond their normal size.

Angelfish

Native to all oceans and fresh water.

Fun Fact- There are freshwater angelfish and marine Angelfish. The female angelfish will lay between 100-1,000 eggs at a time. Both parents will guard the eggs and raise the young fry (babies).

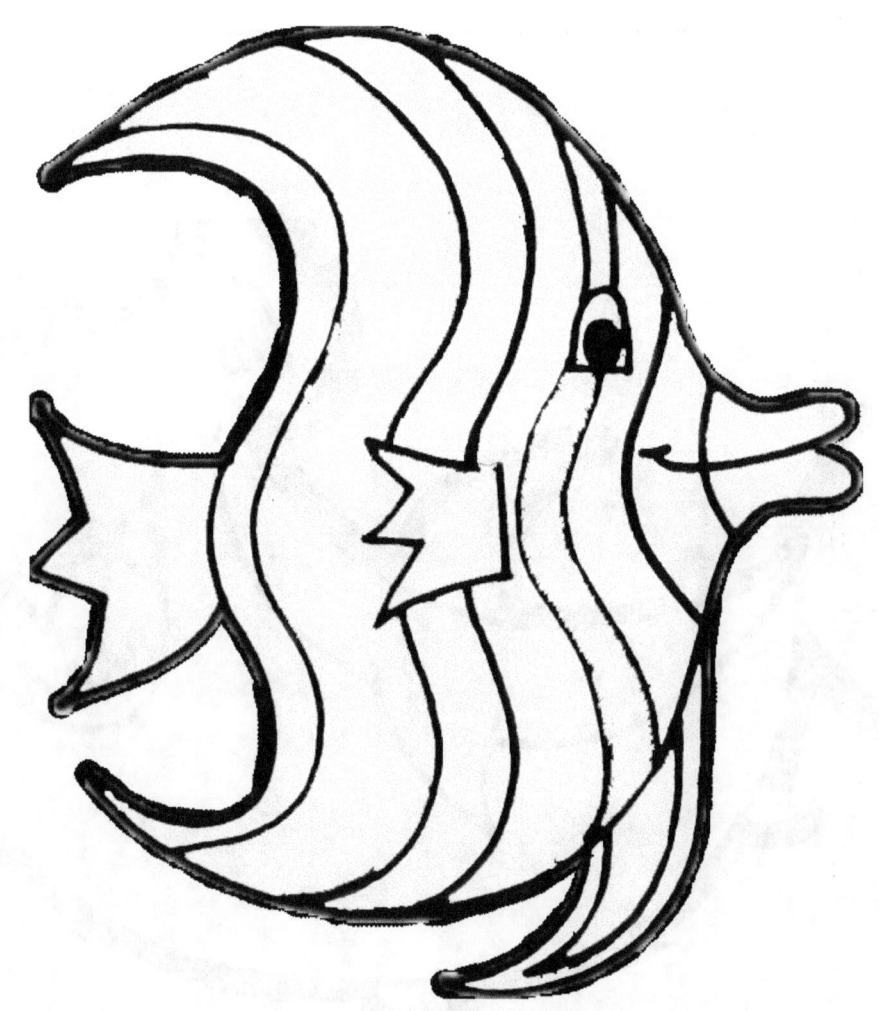

Hammerhead Shark

Native to mild and tropical ocean waters worldwide, far offshore and near shorelines, hammerheads are often seen in mass summer migrations seeking cooler water.

Fun Fact- Hammerheads use their wide heads to attack their favorite meal, the stingray, pinning the ray against the sea floor.

Stingray

Native to shallow coastal ocean waters in mild seas. They spend most of their time inactive, partially buried in sand and only moving with the tide.

Fun Fact- While the stingray's eyes are located on top of its body, the mouth, nostrils, and gill slits are on its underbelly. Many rays have strong jaw teeth that allow them to crush mollusks like clams, oysters, and mussels.

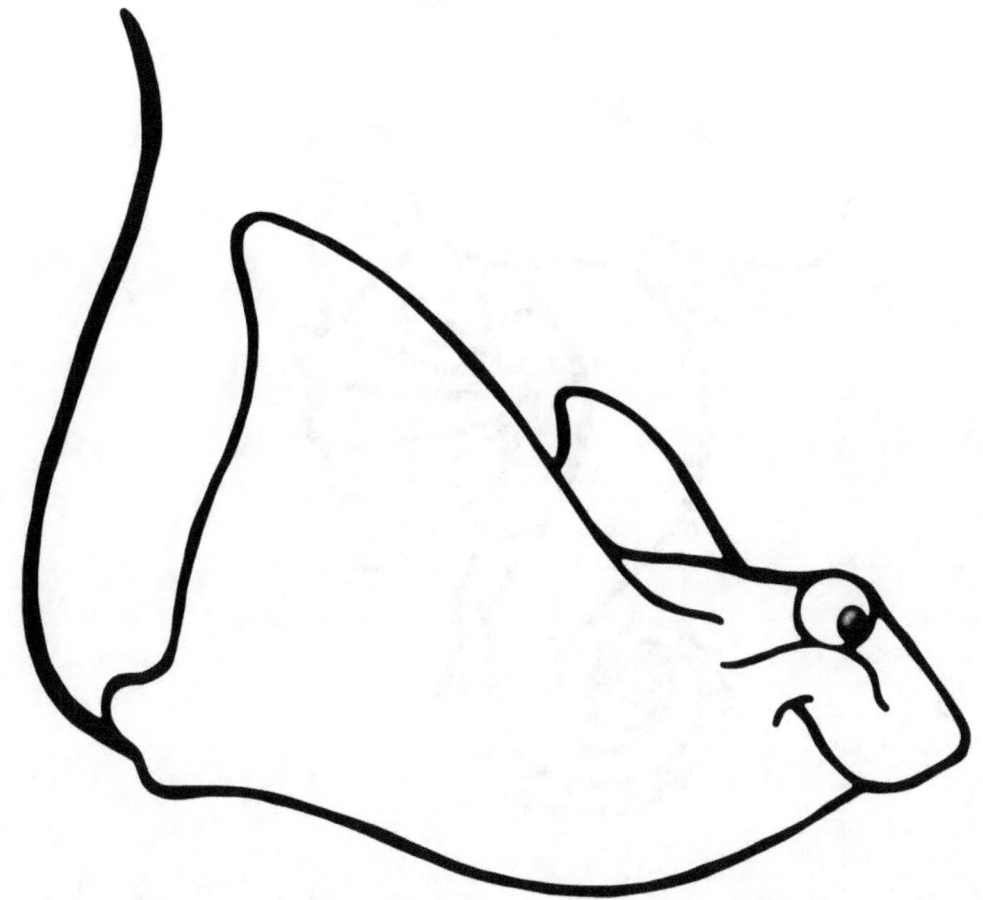

Seahorse

Native to *shallow tropical oceans and temperate waters throughout the world.*

Fun Facts- Seahorses don't have any teeth or stomach. Food passes through their digestive systems so quickly that they must eat almost constantly to stay alive.

Parrotfish

Native to tropical reefs of all the world's oceans.

Fun Facts- Parrotfish have pajamas! Every night, specific species of parrotfish wrap themselves in a transparent cocoon. The cocoon is made of mucous squirted out from an organ on their heads. Scientists think the cocoon hides their scent, making them harder for night-time predators, like moray eels, to find.

Special Writing Pages

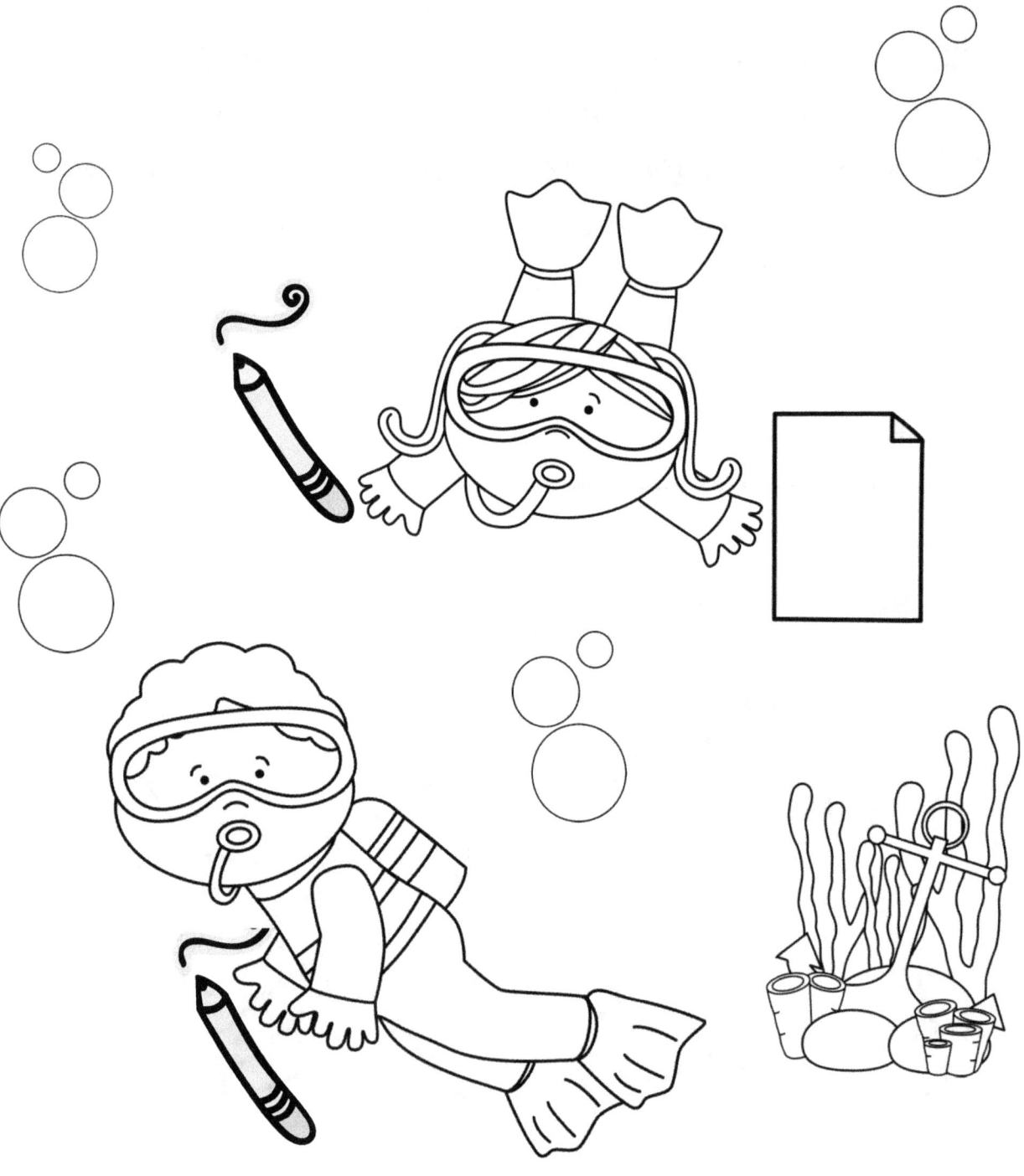

About the Author

Jan May loved homeschooling her two children. Whether it was attending re-enactments of the Revolutionary War or collecting an amphibian zoo, hands-on education was always at the forefront. She is author of the *Creative Writing Made Easy* series that engages even the most reluctant writers! All of these books are filled with fun interactive language activities involving each type of learner: visual, auditory and kinesthetic. Having been a creative writing teacher for over fifteen years, she believes that given the right tools, every child can learn to write and love it!

Visit her website for fun crafts and recipes for kids and for her online schedule inspiring high school teens to deepen their fiction writing. www.NewMillenniumGirlBooks.com

Look for other titles in this series and turn writing time into a delight!

www.ingramcontent.com/pod-product-compliance
Lightning Source LLC
Chambersburg PA
CBHW060517300426
44112CB00017B/2713